CHANTS OF REALISM

ASHFORD LYONETTE

Contents

Contents

Contents

Acknowledgements

I am indebted to my parents, grandparents, sisters, brother, aunts, uncles and relatives; near and far, who have always been a constant source of support. It is from them that I have learned to take one day at a time.

Colleagues and Students who have taught me valuable lessons in our journey together. I extend my wholehearted gratitude to all the people who have touched my life in some way or the other.

My wife, Rachael who has always been the energy and force that drives me. It is her belief in me that convinces me that I am good enough. My daughters, Reanne and Rebecca, for being the reason for my inexhaustible joy.

About The Author

Ashford Lyonette is an English teacher and Senior Master at SelaQui International School. Having traversed many topographies of Life, he has recognised his calling towards Poetry.

Ripened to noon, Ashford believes in embracing all opportunities to augment patience, understanding and wisdom. He too, like every man, has his dreams. His dreams are to be read, spoken of, and remembered. His dreams are for his children, that they are never in want; that they master the art of dealing with triumph and disaster. As Kipling puts it 'treat those two impostors just the same.'

The Education Industry, where he has spent a decade and a half has proved to be a vital platform to mould young minds and touch lives. He sees in his students traces of his own juvenescence. He enjoys the tug-of- war between the brazenness of youth and midlife maturity.

In his arsenal of aptitudes: poetry, music, cooking and biking are forerunners. If there was one last; before the curtains fall, it would undoubtedly be a final recitation of one of his verses to his beloved daughters.

About The Book

Every Art form has its intricacies and every artist renowned to inconspicuous, armed with tools of imagination and skill attempts crafting a masterpiece.

A sequence to the previously published anthology 'Purple Blossom" 2017, **'Chants of Realism'** *is a collection of poems that are harvested from the silk of Life. The silk which is expertly woven by humankind to clothe our starkness.*

The poems, sequenced alphabetically, touch upon the fragile realities of life and relationships. A tinge of humour ensures that we shoulder our yoke with elegance. Reminiscing yester years, we anticipate tomorrow and take the day's weather in our stride. We build bridges and mend walls, criticize success and celebrate falls; resent and forgive, receive and give till we reach the last page; only to realize that we are just like books in a library, some open, some unread.

The latter section of the book is the author's impression of Limerick poetry. A form of traditional humourous lighthearted verse tweaked to a different tune.

1. ANOTHER

Another storm after the calm,
Like laughter after a tear's shed.
An agonising pain, a soothing balm,
The morning sun, a night in bed.
Another triumph after a fall,
Like Nirvana after dreaded death.
Many a swaddling, many a pall,
A time to rejoice a time to regret.
Another sweetheart after a heartache,
Like ebb and flow of the sea.
All is shielded, all's at stake,
Often a prisoner, occasionally free.

2. ANXIETY AND SERENITY

Anxiety and serenity debated,
Inside a muddled mind.
Each of their opinions,
Was certainly well defined.

Anxiety said "I think I feel a weakness,
I'm worried about my health.
I surely must plan my finances,
So my kin has no dearth of wealth."
Serenity said reassuringly,
'Exercise will be a start.
Don't worry about your children,
They'll define their own path.'

Anxiety sighed "What about my rank at work,
And my entitlement to pay.
I wonder if all I've accumulated,
Will be lost some hapless way.?"

Serenity comforted, 'You must toil on,
Believing, every dog has its day.
Remember Life itself is transitory,
And nothing's here to stay.'

Anxiety pined, "Where have the dear dead gone?
What lies in store tomorrow?
All my day is an oscillation,
Between a little joy, much sorrow."

'Cheer up!' exclaimed Serenity,
'Life's too short to pine.
Put on some sanguine lenses,
And all will be just fine.'

3. A PACKET OF CHIPS EACH

Unkempt hair and blistered feet,
Innocence long since lost.
A little urchin roams the street,
In hope to combat cost.
His clothes of neglect loosely fit,
His eyes don't dare to dream.
Armed with premature sharpened wit,
He's learned to plot and scheme.

His brightness meant for the day,
At night, to darkness he must return.
Where unwillingly he gives away,
All that the day could earn.
He was fed on rationed supplies,
In a shanty echoing want.
Sleep evades his tired tries,
For hunger comes to haunt.

I yelled at him when he touched me,
With hands dirtier than contamination.
My privilege knew not his misery,
And hence the retaliation.
My daughter sat in the rear seat,
I adored the way she smiled.
I saw her look at his naked feet,
And realised that he's a child.

In regret, I called him back,
His footsteps to retrace.
His hesitant pace was rather slack,
And panic veiled his face.
I bought for both a packet of chips,
With hope to make amend.
I read a thank you on his silent lips,
Which caused my guilt to end.

4. A SHOP YOU CAN'T AFFORD

This place was peculiar,
For there was nothing on display.
One would think that all the ware,
Was secretly stored away.
Yet there were many people,
That queued in desperate want.
And all of them were wealthy,
With plenty money to flaunt.

But here the trade was different,
You couldn't buy at will.
Each one had to wait their turn,
An application to fill.
If your request fit the cut,
You would be let in.
While all the rejects were brutishly,
Thrown into a bin.

The lucky ones were let in,
For a time that was very short.
So they had to quickly narrow down,
On what was to be bought?
All the goods in boxes,
Neatly were arranged.
The terms displayed distinctly,

'NO EXCHANGE'.

And then there was another catch,
You could not take a look.
Just take a pick of a box,
And pay for what you took.
Cash was not accepted,
You couldn't pay by card.
The tagged price must be paid,
Bargaining was barred.

All the boxes were labeled,
In clear capitalized font.
Each of it so tempting,
All of it you'd want.
Youth was put up for sale,
Acceptance and Peace too.
Eternal Happiness was laid out,
Under the section 'New'.

The highly priced bestsellers,
Were numbered one, two, three.
Three was Wisdom, two Freedom,
And one was Immortality.

But none of the clients,
The quoted price could pay.
For who would donate their wealth,
Break ties and walk away.

Wishful people come and go,
Yet sales are never made.
Most claim the deal is flawed,
To guise that they're afraid.
And so their lives in shackles are,
Each one of the horde.
The exhibits stay unclaimed,
For no man can afford.

5. AT GALWAN VALLEY

He was a shade of yellow, I a bit bronze,
Both in uniforms with lesser pros more cons.
I claimed to be a patriot; he said so was he,
Each staking claim to disputed territory.

I held the tricolor; he made me see red,
From a simple soul emerged a griffin head.
A river flowed below, mountains rose above,
The air was too frigid for the passing of a dove.

What was once banter turned to furious fray,
Neither I nor he chose to walk away.
We were hailed as martyrs both him and me,
And granted our share of land, spanning eight by three.

Top brass on either side is bent on keeping tally,
An eye for an eye, tooth for tooth at Galwan Valley

6. AT THE CEMETERY

A candle burns upon your grave,
A ray of hope in deathly air.
That melting wax works its way,
Like my tears of despair.

Upon the mound, a cross affixed,
For peace that is eternal.
I guise well the struggle to cope,
With the void that is internal.

Childhood comes back in a flash,
Playful day and peaceful night.
Joy was found in simple things,
Like shadows formed by candlelight.

Letters that the postman brought,
Written at a different latitude.
Yuletide's festive feel,
Nightly prayers of gratitude.

Your genius I see in my children,
As I closely watch them grow.
They draw, paint, run and sing,
Though the artist is no more.

When the present pauses briefly,
A present that's fleeting fast.
I often flip in my mind,
Those albums of the past.

7. BUILDING BRIDGES

Of all those bridges we've built,
Gradually or in frantic haste.
Only a few stand the test of time,
Most disintegrate and are replaced.

Replaced by another bridge,
That two islands link.
Sentiments pace to and fro,
Faster than one can think.

Think of the congested traffic,
That the bridge withstood.
And though it wanted to resign,
It absorbed all it could.

Could a bridge bear burden,
If it were not for human will.
For even when overladen,
The bridge still sensed some thrill.

The thrill of obligation,
That comes to us in birth.
Of goodwill and envy,
That tells us what we're worth.

• 13 •

The worth of every bridge,
By cost cannot be told.
So build your bridges wisely,
For only some will hold.

8. CAMOUFLAGE AND MIMICRY

Just like a colour changing chameleon,
Or a Polar bear that blends with the snow.
Every one of the world's eight billion,
Use camouflage to hide or show,
The anxiety, the stress, the addiction,
Concealed with emotions quite fake.
Appeasement, truce or friction,
Impels to cling to, or forsake.

Mimicry comes at a tender age,
From parental posture, manner and style.
In calmness or agitated rage,
Depicted by furrowed brow or smile.
What they see is what they learn,
In the book of life pages don't unturn.

9. COMING FULL CIRCLE

Moist like a dew kissed petal,
Lay hidden by Winter's frost;
The radiance of infant innocence,
For adolescence desires are lost.

Bolder than brass about decisions,
Without resistance and fears.
Adulthood takes over adolescence,
When mistakes are regretted through tears.

A maestro in all magnificence,
Orchestrates the tune and the song.
Making the most of Life's rhythms,
For ageing will soon come along.

Old and wrinkled like crumpled paper,
longing for company and love.
A being as shrewd as a serpent,
Is now docile as a dove.

10. COMMON THINGS

A chair, a bed,
Words often said.
A pan, a plate,
Rage born out of hate.
Are all too common things.

Disease and stress,
The opinionated press.
Meth and vape,
Barbaric rape.
Are all too common things.

Weeds and Moss,
The win, the loss.
What's earned and spent,
Blasphemy and sacrosanct.
Are all too common things.

A ring, a pin,
Deceit and sin.
Grief and mirth,
Like death and birth.
Are all too common things.

11. COMMERCIAL GOD

Where miracles happen and dreams are dreamt,
In faith was constructed a monument.
Believers came with offerings in prayer,
And thronged a multitude filled with despair.

Testimonies of healing spread far and wide,
The delivered bowed in reverence and cried.
Some priests held fort as the crowds grew,
While draftsmen drew plans for constructions new.

Hotels and eateries to cater to the masses,
Devotees must queue if they haven't got passes.
Pilgrimage packages on hoardings displayed,
Offerings recycled; priestly services paid.

Faith and fervour competes with fraud,
For man has succeeded in commercialising God.

12. DREAMS, HOPES, MIRACLES

The yoke upon his shoulder,
Borne to plough his land.
Dreaming of his harvest,
While sowing seeds by hand.

A net cast out before dawn,
From a boat deep at sea.
The sun angled above the mast,
The catch comes patiently.

Bread and fish multiplied,
A multitude to feed.
Fish caught in a net of hope,
Bread born from the dreams of a seed.

13. FILM FAIR

The red carpet's rolled,
reporters are live,
Catching up with celebrities,
As they arrive.
Their expensive apparels,
exorbitantly costly cars.
The layman queues,
for a glimpse of the stars.
Stars whose skeletons,
are in closets protected,
leaving the paparazzi dejected.
They wave their hands,
and join their palms.
A Pout, A smile,
to flaunt their charms.
Oddity of speech and practice,
Brands them actor and actress.
Will you not agree,
To their privileged pedigree?
Just one forgotten fact,
We pay to watch them act.

14. FIND TIME

I've bartered youth for insight,
And reached the seventh stage,
My frail limbs have no might,
Yet no number my soul can cage.

Neither appetite for food nor wealth,
Like when I was in my prime,
Need not you pity my failing health,
Just spare me some of your time.

I'd like to talk of days gone by,
Of trails I've maneuvered through.
I earnestly need to justify,
What I couldn't have done for you.

My coffers are not overflowing,
I have no legacy will,
It's your presence that sees me glowing,
And my empty spaces fill.

My epitaph I will not read,
Nor hear the eulogy you say.
My clock ticks an unbridled speed,
Find Time for me today.

15. FOOLISH FAIRYTALES

Cinderella got her name from cinders,
King Arthur's favourite was Tom Thumb.
The wolf disguised in grandma's clothing,
Proves Red Riding Hood was quite dumb.

The three pigs tried their hand at masonry,
Rapunzel's hair was cut by the witch.
The emperor was draped in finest fabric
That the swindling weavers didn't stitch.

The three billy goats made it across the bridge,
A poisoned apple caused Snow White to sleep.
The queen didn't know Rumpelstiltskin's name,
So fear of losing her first born made her weep.

Goldilocks ate the little bear's porridge,
Jack followed the giant up the beanstalk.
The Prince's love for Aurora,
Had Sleeping Beauty rise and walk.

16. FOOL'S PARADISE

Once upon a time,
In a land without a name.
There lived a thriving tribe,
Domesticated and tame.
There wasn't social structure,
No economic divide.
No one knew of envy,
Let alone of pride.
No walls fringed houses,
No property dispute.
No cases thus no courts,
No lawyer's refute.

Was it some invasion?
By some alien race.
That bestowed negativity,
And robbed them their grace.
Neighbours became strangers,
Relatives started to compete.

Man and money synonymous,
Children taught deceit.
Religious fervour fragmented,
Like when Babel fell.
What probably once was Eden,
Some serpents altered to Hell

17. GRANDPA'S CANDIES

"If forgiveness was sweet candy,
You could buy it at the store.
And hand it out bigheartedly,
So bitter tongues wag no more.

Yet before you extend generously,
Be sure to take a bite,
For who's to know the sweetness,
Might just set you right.

I never did like candies,
Not even as a child.
As a boy I thought it sassy,
When a man I found them mild.

As I turned old, I realized,
There's more than meets the eye.
Some candies are so delectable,
That it can make you cry.

I gave them to old colleagues,
Who've retired just like me.
All our grudges were dissolved,
We were purged of misery.

I shared it with my neighbour,
We'd been loggerheads for years.
He ate it with much relish,
As his eyes brimmed with tears.

When grandma was sick one night,
I gave her a candy, with my best smile.
She clenched it in her feeble palm, saying,
'It took you quite a while'.

Your father is a busy man,
Who hasn't much time for me.
But he faithfully comes once a fortnight,
For his share of MY candy.

For the Sunday Offertory,
I charitably offered a few.
And later at the Confessional, whispered,
'Father you can have one too.'

A pocket full of candies,
To forgive and to forget.
Wouldn't cost you much at all,
But will save you much regret.

Blinded by loathe my entire life,
It took my declining sight to see.
That the very first of those candies,
Should have been eaten by me,"

18. GRANNY AND THE PESTS

A mouse scurried across the floor,
In haste to meet his Misses.
And those squeaks behind the door.
Were actually their kisses.

A lizard crawled along the wall,
His tail an old man's hunch.
And gobbled down a flea quite small,
For it was time for lunch.

Some mosquitoes flew into the room,
As the window nets were porous.
Bloodthirsty faces wore no gloom,
They swarmed around in chorus.

Ants queued in shiny sheen,
In collaboration they worked.
Toiling endlessly for their queen,
Who did nothing all day but twerked.

Chestnut cockroaches are a creep,
That hide in all strange places.
Like phantoms roam while we sleep,
Leaving behind no traces.

Pest Control took all the pains,
They sprayed every nook and cranny.
Now all but one pest remains,
To pester old, angry granny.

19. HOLLOW MEN

Hello men! yes you hollow men,
When, when, when,
Will you wake from your sleep?
Throw tantrums or weakly weep,
In acknowledgment of being a slave,
From cradle to grave.
To wanting and spending,
Borrowing and lending,
Attacking and defending,
Avoiding and blending,
Breaking and mending,
A masquerade unending.
In Life's hollow symphony,
Mortal men are never free.

20. IDIOMATICALLY SPEAKING

"Well I'm going to hit the sack",
Said a shepherd to his sheep.
What he was actually telling them,
Was that he was going to sleep.

"Doctor! I'm under the weather",
Exclaimed Moby Dick.
On examination it was verified,
That he was very sick.

"We've broken new ground",
Edmund and Tenzing declared.
For they had achieved a feat,
That no one before had dared.

The other night at the party,
Tom Sawyer was on cloud nine.
The morning revealed his happiness,
Was due to an overdose of wine.

Chief Geronimo was known for,
His blows of hot and cold.
His swing in mood and being rude,
were attributed to him growing old.

Those that know to cut corners,
Is the employer's favourite worker.
They retain him for he saves cost,
Ignoring his being a shirker.

Soldiers kept on their toes,
No it wasn't any ballet dance.
They were alert and attentive,
So that the king could prance.

21. IN THE GENES

At track and field excels.
Beware of the wizard's kin,
Who knows to curse and spell.

• 32 •

22. JUST ACROSS THE ROAD

Just across the road I see,
A hapless lad in misery.
Hunger all over his face,
Yet his smile has some grace.
Reluctant to ask for charity,
Compelled by life's disparity,
He stretches out his arm.

Just across the road I see,
A car that spells luxury.
From open sunroof a head springs,
And the wind, what thrill brings.
Joyous laughter, carefree look,
A Lays packet in his hand he took,
And threw it in the street.

Just across the road I see,
The famished boy brim with glee.
He grabbed the packet in hasty wit,
And relished every remaining bit.
In a jiffy he licked it clean,
Then starved eyes and frame lean,
Looked up to thank the sky.

Just across the road I see,
A world void of symmetry.
A ravenous boy, another content,
One craving food, one merriment.
One malnourished, the other well-fed,
Then in gratitude I bowed my head,
Thankful for my means.

23. KITES

Exhausted by monotony,
I set out on a drive.
Surely there was no hurry,
For I had nowhere to arrive.
Detouring off the trodden roads,
I entered country land.
Distant expanses in tints of green,
Wherever the eyes scanned.

A carrot sun, half hidden,
Behind a mountaintop.
Caused the sky to flush a bit,
And prompted me to stop.
Birds in flight; returning,
Before the fall of night.
Two twin looking little boys,
Stared skyward at their kite.

Marveling at the majestic wings,
They lent to it direction.
Little hands released then pulled,
The thread with such perfection.

The fearless kite rode the sky,
'To rise' it's sole intention.
Higher and higher it ascended,
In the wind's genial attention.

A wail of a worried woman,
Had the boys alert.
Hurriedly they rolled the spool,
And brought the kite to earth.
Befuddled, the light - headed kite,
Could not comprehend.
Why it's basking glory,
Was abruptly put to end?

Frivolous thoughts came to mind,
As the boys were homeward bound.
Are we kites on someone's thread,
Pompously flying around?
Soaring high, against the sky,
For all the world to see.
Forgetting that we're tethered,
By strings of destiny.

24. KNOWING DADDY

I never understood Daddy for he was always stern,
Why was he always hoarding every pie he'd earn?
He had an Atlas cycle, the milkman had one too,
Why was he so miserly to resole a worn out shoe?

I never understood why he often borrowed, seldom spent,
Why he'd feed beggars each Friday during Lent?
Mercy church his retreat, his mother's house his haunt,
Was it Christ or his mother who bailed him out of want?

Father's constant nagging and worry, I cannot comprehend,
Through school, college, work, his advice would never end.
Does he confuse a grown up man to be his little boy?
Even when I moved away, his calls they did annoy.

A decade and two daughters later, now I understand,
Father wanted to be Best Daddy; yet none of it was planned.

25. LABELS

A talkative one is labeled,
'Ms. Know it all.'
A 'dwarf' or a 'midget,'
Is one who's built is small.
The ones that like to taste success,
Are tagged as 'ambitious.'
And everyone must be aware,
Of that spiteful 'Mr. Vicious.'
The one that does not socialize,
Is classified as 'Introvert.'
If you're attractive or attract,
You'll be branded 'Flirt.'
The one that likes to have his way,
Is categorized as 'bossy.'
Denizens from down under,
Are referred to as 'Aussie.'
'Misers' are tightfisted,
For the do not like to spend.
'Grumblers' are kept at arm's length,
For their complains never end.
Those that defy authority,
Are termed a 'Rebel.'
'Humble' are the individuals,
That do but never tell.
'Orthodox' is the classification,

For the rigid sort of folk.
'Sensitive' are those,
That cannot take a joke.
'Butterfingers' are people,
Very clumsy with things.
Small minded 'Pompous' men,
Like to believe they're kings.

26. LOST IN THE VOID

Riot and strike have started to spike,
Human rights is a growing concern.
But for poor folk, all this is a joke,
They're consumed day wages to earn.

Articles abolished, shrines demolished,
Under threat the minority tribes.
But for rich bloke, they verdicts revoke,
They've stacked surplus for bribes.

Votes and ranks, paying up banks,
At retirement a burnt body relaxes.
Bourgeois chaps, caught in traps,
Their earnings consumed by taxes.

27. MAN TO MOTHER

Cradle me again,
Comfort me when I cry.
I want to feel special,
The apple of your eye.

Cajole my faltering,
Coax my strength.
Hear me patiently,
When I talk at length.

Ruffle my hair,
Put me to bed.
May all my afflictions,
Abandon my head.

Take from me man,
And make me a boy.

28. MISFIT MEN

There's a race of misfit men,
Some only talk now and then.
They look away and seldom stare,
And sit askew on a straight back chair.
Some like to keep to solitude,
And none can tell their actual mood.
Their ideas they rarely share,
And worry less about what to wear.

Some call them geek some call them gawk,
Some say they have a mental block.
They like to read and like to think,
A compliment can make them sink.
Some are calm others like trouble,
Some guzzle their scotch on the double.
They don't want to marry, they like to be free,
Some like to indulge in a spending spree.

Some muse over death, some over life,
Some want a man to be their wife.
There are those orthodox to the core,
And others who's swag you cannot ignore.
Some like to drift in fancy cars,

Some have not a farthing but act like the stars.
Feared are the ones angry and rude,
Everyone avoids the ones who brood.

There are those with a voracious appetite,
And others whose existence is owed to spite.
Some like their fingers in every pie,
Some window shop but never buy.
Some that preach and others that pray,
Some that cast the demons away.
Yet each insist that they belong,
Oblivious to anything being wrong.

29. MS. PREJUDICE

Ms. Prejudice must be everywhere,
Against dark skin, opposing blond hair.
She has critical views on choice of faith,
And a demarcation based on social state.

At times her bias is based on gender,
An unborn fetus seen as offender.
She calls races yellow, races white,
Jews and gentiles she imbues with spite.

In youth she tends to scorn the old,
With age she wants the youth to mould.
She takes immense pride about her nation,
And cares little for global deprivation.

I wonder if you've ever been in her shoes,
For in constricting spaces negativity brews.

30. OPPORTUNITY

When you're indecisive,
And a choice is to be made.
The tempting path is taken,
Discomfort to evade.
Safe spaces satisfy,
Why then take a chance,
And find yourself offside,
After giving up your stance.
Weighing the stakes and gain,
You might just rethink.
For opportunity knocks once,
To vanish in a blink.

31. PEOPLE FALL OUT

People fall out for many a reason,
Like altered moods with a change of season.
Trivial things have the ego spurred,
Daggers drawn; dialogue differed.

'I'm convinced I am right; They must admit,
My intelligence surpasses their common wit.'
Each one's thought echoes the same,
'It isn't me but them to blame.'

Consistent time continues to pace,
Avoidance and indifference take up space,
Between two individuals, both puppets of fate,
Each for the other's apology wait.

People fall out, move on, don't reconcile,
Though forgiveness costs a simple smile.

32. PHOBIATIC

Father Gilligan got tongue tied at every sermon,
Glossophobia was diagnosed.
For his fear of public speaking,
The parish church was closed.

Aquaphobia caused Henry to avoid bathing,
He suffered rashes and matted locks.
Because of his irrational fear of water,
He smelled like dirty socks.

Oscar now a barber,
Took time identifying.
That aerophobia was the cause,
To give up his profession of flying.

Bibliophobic Jacob was oft laughed at,
For he couldn't read a line.
For fear of books he dropped out of school,
And now he slaughters swine.

Betty was chromophobic,
A fear that keeps colours at bay.
She only dressed in black and white,
Wearing not even a shade of gray.

Stanley is fifty-three and single,
Gamophobia was the cause.
But he smiles satisfaction,
When others grumble about in-laws.

Jack became a doctor,
Despite his fear of being ill.
Hypochondriac Jack was a quack,
Now know as 'Dr. Kill'.

Mike Morgan was a midget,
Naturally, he found things too large.
Megatophobic Mike used all his skill,
And built his palace in a garage.

Anna Jane ate very little,
For fear of gaining weight.
Obesophobic Anna is thin as a twig,
And has trouble finding a date.

108 year old Dave may never die,
Thanatophobia has seized his brain.
His fear of death is so intense,
That he smiles through the ageing strain.

33. QUEST

In quest of greener pastures,
The bleating sheep did flock.
Expectantly moving forward,
With no one taking stock.
Akin to a misinterpreted mirage,
The other side seemed green.
The herd yearned the Utopian garden,
No simple sheep had seen.

As the flock paced forward,
Their destiny to breach.
The greener grass kept advancing,
And was always out of reach.
Worn out to exhaustion,
The simple sheep gave up the quest.
They settled by the churchyard,
And lay themselves to rest.

34. RECIPES

A recipe my mother taught me,
In no cookbook could I find.
It has two basic ingredients,
Forgiveness and being kind.

My father was no master chef,
Yet he taught me a recipe too.
A combination of two items,
Of being humble and true.

A recipe I've known from grandpa,
Can be found beneath the crust.
It comprises of three key elements,
Honesty, loyalty and trust.

My grandma taught me a recipe,
That has nothing to do with food.
Yet I find it quite flavoursome,
To be courageous and prude.

If you've known of these ingredients,
Then take them off the shelf.
Blend them in equal portions,
For mastery of the self.

35. REVOLT

"Do not compel us ," he pleaded
"Please Lord! don't compel us," he refrained.
But his advice was taken for arrogance,
By order he had him restrained.

"You're on our land" they said
"You must respect our Faith."
He followed the Company's orders.
And welcomed none of the debate.

Then one soldier spoke up: saying,
He'd never the cartridge bite.
The Brits resistance insisted,
That they were all power and might.

A Mutiny was soon to follow,
With revolt and rebellion displayed.
And all that fear of the Company,
Gradually started to fade.

Unsettled by Western Education,
Vexed by the Doctrine of Lapse.
Taxes, economic hardship and cartridges,
Caused the Company to collapse.

36. SNAKES AND LADDERS

Who is it that plays
Dice with our lives?
Our pace determined by the
toss they throw.
Our ascent and descent
Success and strife,
All at the mercy of
some maestro.
Ladders climbed; Snakes
bring us down.
The gamut experienced
Smile to frown,
Over and Over
till the Finish.

37. SETTING SAIL

Into a sea of opportunity,
Michael set out to sail.
He was not bound by direction,
For seas don't have a trail.

The rising sun was soothing,
The air a faint breeze.
The ocean waters placid,
He felt himself at ease.

Many nautical miles later,
When the sun was overhead,
He thumped his chest with pride,
'I'm progressing,' he said.

It was not until the evening,
When the winds began to wail.
Which caused his boat to rock,
And turned his courage pale.

By night the waves threatened,
No direction could be found.
He desperately needed to anchor,
And get back on solid ground.

When all hope was almost lost,
His compass came to mind.
He hastily put the thing to use,
A safe harbour to find.

In that dark treacherous hour,
He realized what he had.
The safe harbour was his home,
The compass, mom and dad.

38. SOWING SEEDS

When you sow your seeds on barren land,
And imprudence believes that they shall bloom.
No saviour can reverse what you've planned,
So sooner than later you'll meet with gloom.

If you sow those seeds on rocky bed,
With a conviction that a plant will sprout.
You must consider them as good as dead,
A sprightly seed will succumb to drought.

If you plant your seeds on fertile silt,
Quite soon you will see them shoot.
With a little heed and a little toil,
Your labour will flourish and bear fruit.

39. TEN TERRORISTS

Ten men were chosen,
They were sure to pick the best.
And train them for a mission,
That promised eternal rest.

Their weapons keen and polished,
Their views indoctrinated.
They wore smiles of conviction,
Knowing well what was fated.

By sea they came the ten of them,
Spilling blood in salty water.
Firing round of indiscriminate bullets,
At man, wife, son and daughter.

They lay siege on the city,
Cafe, hospital, hotels, station.
Death danced in rage and fury,
Sadists rejoiced the culmination.

Three days it took the nation's bravest,
This barbaric act to halt.
A hundred and seventy lives lost,
In a planned, inhumane assault.

A bloodbath of a mission,
Nine died, one was caught.
A fortune spent on security,
Before to justice he was brought.

No creed teaches any man,
To use violence to intimidate.
Every shrine echoes petitions,
For terrorism to abate.

40. TENDER TUNES

Waking up to a repetitive tune,
That out of the blue comes to mind.
Like walking on an endless dune,
It plays on automated rewind.

Sometimes its a chant of praise,
Devotees call it psalm or hymn.
That makes you reflect on your ways,
Causing the subdued guilt to brim.

Familiar melodies of youth when sound,
They transport you to a forgotten past.
Then priceless recollections come around,
With a futile want for them to last.

Sentimental are those refrains,
Special to one whose end is met,
It brings along tears and quiet pain,
With memories one can't forget.

41. THE ALTAR

Rouge carnations in vases,
The altar linen immaculate white.
A baptismal font in glistening gold,
On a morning jovial and bright.
An infant baptised and christened,
In faith of the Redeemer's light.

Red roses adorn the pew,
Right along the aisle.
A bridal veil, a nuptial trail,
The congregation wears a smile.
Rings exchanged and vows spoken,
To walk the eternal mile.

White lily wreaths atop a coffin,
Lamentation annihilates mirth.
The eulogy read, recalling the dead,
Mortal remains returned to earth.
The Saviour called on one last time,
In resurrection or rebirth.

42. THE LION'S REIGN

The lion's pride was coronated,
And proclaimed mayor of the city.
The serpent hissed in evil envy,
Sighing "Isn't that a pity."

The lion read the rules,
To the confused common crowd.
Though the directive was dictatorial,
It was his; of that he was proud.

All creatures in groups segregated,
And assigned a specific task.
While the others went to work,
The lion lay down to bask.

A scurry of squirrels gathered nuts,
The bulls' stubbornness ploughed on.
Rabbits architected safe tunnels,
Giraffes kept watch; dusk to dawn.

Elephants paved the vital paths,
Grumbling beavers did the construction.
The lion preyed on the feebler lot,
And was given to consumption.

Wolves and hyenas roamed in packs,
An anarchy was brewing.
Yet the lion's prudence was convinced,
He knew what he was doing.

The lion roared in arrogance,
About his critical view.
He told the other animals,
What he thought was true.

In time the lion grows old and slow,
The citizens conflicted.
A proficient mane took up the reign,
And the lion was evicted.

The hyenas laughed, bulls bellowed,
Squirrels snorted in trivial talk.
It caused them much amusement,
To watch the new male's ceremonious walk.

Kingdoms are lost, kings fall,
They knew this was very true.
The lion would lead for some time,
To be replaced by someone new.

43. THE MAN ON THE CROSS

Ignatius' Society of Jesuits,
Mother Teresa's wrinkles of hope,
Padre Pio's stigmata,
In the Vatican, the Pope.
All embodiment of piety,
In service void of profit or loss,
Reverence to a carpenter's son,
The man upon the cross.

For commoners like you and me,
Life her woes on our brows emboss,
From ecstasy to agony,
Our journey like pitch-and-toss,
Aided by our secret whispers,
To that man upon the cross.

44. THE PLAYGROUND

My children in the playground is the best time of my day,
Oh! If I could teach them Life while they were still at play.
I watch them on the see-saw, fluctuate up then down,
And wildly spin fearlessly on the thrilling merry go round.

They hastily climb the ladder then slide back to the sand,
Sometimes suffering abrasions when awkwardly they land.
The labyrinth jungle gym makes the climb confusing,
To reach the top or risk the fall constantly a musing.

Alone on the park bench sometimes; seeking solitude,
A lack of will crafted by an inexplicable change in mood.
Oscillating on the swing, a pleasant wind does blow,
A push causing elevation, a drag making it slow.

When their mirthful spirits surge forth in sportive spree,
I'd tell them 'Life's a playground; Bethlehem to Calvary.'

45. THE PHANTOM AND THE PRIEST

One moonlit night a spirit,

Set out on a haunting spree.

Of course he was bored to death,

By the silence at the cemetery.

He sallied past a drunkard,

Who staggered his home to find,

But the drunk thought the specter,

Was a craft of his sozzled mind.

Then he tried to scare a madman,

Who on the pavement naked lay.

The madman's face turned frenzied,

And the phantom flew away.

He finally found his victim,

To whom the night's amusement he owed.

For as the apparition altered and wailed,

A cassock ran down the road.

The next morning behind the altar,

The sexton got a fright.

For in the tabernacle was parish priest,

His face, Eucharist white.

The parish priest was speechless,
His joints as stiff in death.
His cassock crushed and stained,
His undergarments soaking wet.

The Bishop was then sent for,
To anoint the ailing priest.
It was then he gathered courage,
To talk of the dreadful beast.

The investigation revealed,
What caused the priest a shock,
The ghost it seemed had taken,
His cassock to be a frock.

46. THE SECOND WAVE

Whilst the devastating diagnosis rampantly spreads,
The nation frantically feuds for oxygen and hospital beds.
Most journeys are short lived, from ICU to mortuary,
For living hearts are arrested while eternal souls set free.

Corpses wait outside the crematorium, a token for a turn,
Even the dead are patient for their mortal remains to burn.
Others' grief broadcasted, an insecure country seems stirred,
The opposition tactically tweets; our leader says not a word.

Mothers mourn, children cry, widows, widowers wail,
Along the sacrosanct Ganges abandoned bodies sail.
Condolences cannot comfort the loss of a dearly loved one,
Neither psychic nor mystic can have the agony undone.

Dehydrated through tears, when life comes to a standstill,
We must pray for the departed and surrender to God's will.

47. THE TONGUE

There is a tongue inside my head,
That starts to talk when I lie in bed.
Its interrogative tone of what, why, when,
Makes me analyze event, time, men.

What went wrong? Why couldn't I see?
When are happier times destined to be?
Politics in camaraderie so hard to spot,
Hostility remembered and goodwill forgot.

Mistakes of yore that've made me wise,
Memories of loved ones that betray the eyes.
Vacillating between regret and rejoice,
I blame it on fate, though they say it is choice.

Scrutiny spent, I close my heavy eyes,
Anticipating the morrow's sun will rise.

48. THE TREE

Logged down for timber,
a bed, a chair to make.
My shady expanse uprooted,
There must be some mistake.

For years on end, I've been a friend,
Yet now I'm just dead wood,
Barren is that land on which,
Once mightily I stood.

The birds chirp rather restlessly,
Like a log to watch me lie,
Perhaps they grieve a haven lost,
And have come to say goodbye.

My limbs they've amputated,
My bark does varnish veil,
A price tag upon my body,
They've put me up for sale.

My race is rapidly reducing,
Bamboo, oak, and teak,
We want to warn of impending doom,
Alas! We cannot speak.

I've been bought, I must go,
Some dwelling to adorn,
They marvel at my present form,
Though my soul is long since gone.

49. THERE'S ALWAYS HOPE

From fragmented faith of yesterday
the morning's hope does rise
Though the path of righteousness
Is no easy compromise

Malice, envy, and egotism
May stop you in your track
Only lenses of optimism
Can cope with such setback

Be not afraid of those who judge
For they must be insecure
Put down that baggage of grudge
Let mind and heart be pure

Though not rewarded or treated right
Be patient and labour on
For darkness only rules the night
And surrenders at the break of dawn

50. THEY TOO

They too cry those burly men,
With moustache pride upon upper lip.
They too wince those that orders give,
When favourable times take a dip.

They too feel the pain of separation,
When precious ones part ways.
Though their stern visage holds well,
You'll sense in their vacant gaze.

They too need to be understood,
Just as they try to understand.
They long for a touch on their shoulders,
A touch of a reassuring hand.

They too need your approval,
Perhaps some validation now and then.
Yet they pretend to be indifferent,
Maybe because they are men.

They too know when they are wrong,
And honestly repent deep inside.
But they refrain from saying "sorry",
To keep their manly pride.

They too feel the stress, the struggle,
When strenuous times prevail.
Yet they'll stoop not to ask for help,
And compromise the Alpha Male.

They too accommodate and sacrifice,
Wearing a smile, just like you.
And whisper your thoughts in their minds,
"Oh! How I wish they knew".

51. UNCROWNED QUEEN

The umbilical cord detached, a bond is fortified,
In the painful hour of birth, a mother's joy cried.
Her arms a cradle, her breasts her newborn's feed,
Her little wants forgotten, to provide all they need.
Her cautious eye observes their crawl, their walk.
She smiles in adoration to hear their gibberish talk.

A trusted confidant to the adolescent's wavering mind,
To all their shortcomings she's oft knowingly blind.
She celebrates their victories and masks their defeat,
Convinces them they're good enough to get back on their feet.
At times she's restrictive and talks a tongue that's stern,
Its just another way in which she expresses her concern.

Her experience teaches to tackle relationships fragile,
And even in family turmoil to wear a reassuring smile.
When age defies the body and she turns feeble and gray,
She might not seem to do much though faithfully she'd pray.
She wears no crown, has no scepter, sits on no throne,
But doesn't she deserve it all for her heart that's careworn?

52. WHAT ARE YOU WOMAN?

What are you woman?
Fragrant, fertile, free,
Carved in leisurely time.
Beguiling beauty at best,
Aphrodite in her prime.

What are you woman?
Uncertain, veiled, knotted,
Walking around sacred fire.
Committing for a lifetime,
Abandoning all self desire.

What are you woman?
Joyous tears in painful birth,
Devoted to raising your young.
Proud of each of their actions,
Not bitter about being unsung.

What are you woman?
Societal anklets of obligation,
A tiara of tormented thought.
Draped in a mantel of compromise,
Walking the ramp of thy lot.

53. WHEN TWO WORLDS COLLIDE

A raven perched on a conifer tree,
Belligerently black as ebony.
Harbinger of the ill to be,
Death, decay, catastrophe.

A dove perched on a mulberry tree,
Pure and mild as infancy.
Denoting peace and spirituality,
Preaching to man morality.

The scavenging raven let out a croak,
An ordinary day to provoke.
Somewhere in Palestine patience broke,
Displacing a multitude of Israeli folk.

The miraculous white dove let out a coo,
As if urging the nations two.
To bury the hatchet and start a new,
For now, calling ceasefire will do.

54. WHEN YOU HIT ROCK BOTTOM

When you hit rock bottom and things are beyond control,
Let not the gloom consume you and take the hope from your soul.
Think of the smiles and laughter; think of the people you've met.
Believe that there will be tomorrow, a tomorrow you wouldn't regret.

Give to none permission with scorn to shatter your faith,
Turn deaf to those schemers , yet make no allowance for hate.
Be proud of those scars in your bosom, they make you just who you are,
Life's riddles and jostles are measures that give you the strength to go far.

Abandoned by near and dear ones, when you find no shoulder to cry,
Look yourself in the mirror, and whisper 'Hey there, let's try.'
Face fear with the spirit of a martyr, failure embrace with a smile.
Stay calm in those moments of trial, for struggle just lasts for a while.

Draw out from the wells of courage, the power to endure the dark,
Strike at the shackles that bind you, cause them to let out a spark.
Remember that you are extraordinary, down till your last breath,
So put on your armour of confidence, for none can defy you but death.

55. WORLDLY WAY

All marvel at the monument,
Who looks at a pillar or a beam?
All praise is for the Captain,
Few recognise the Team.

If all the Team is Captain,
The arrangement fails to run.
For debates are held and minutes kept,
Yet little work gets done.

Hierarchy must be followed,
For all men, helm to deck.
A seasoned squad knows too well,
The noose around the Captain's neck.

56. LIMERICK POETRY

ADOLESCENCE

Adolescence is no position,

To charter out a mission.

For emotions and thoughts,

Are patches and blots,

Seeking recognition.

ALLURING DECEPTION

Don't you think I've forgotten?

Your skin as soft as cotton,

Those eyes of teal blue,

The truth I wish I knew,

Your love would turn me rotten.

ANTONY AND CLEOPARTA

Antony's heart was on fire,

Cleopatra his only desire.

Passion raged on,

Three children were born.

He neglected the Roman Empire.

BACKSTABBERS

Unpredictability is a human fact,
Though in time you've learned the tact,
And just when you think you know,
Which one's a friend which foe,
They stab you in the back.

BEAUTY AND THE PRIEST

Beauty bewedded the beast,
Who hosted a fabulous feast.
But later that night,
Quite literally out of fright,
Beauty eloped with the priest.

BETRAYED

When your wrecked and broken,
at the malign that's spoken,
by trusted folk, you hold dear,
it makes you want to shed a tear,
Hold! Exult! for you've woken.

CONFIDENTIALITY

Confidentiality is meant to rumour,
For work-time intermittent humour.
More contagious than a yawn,
It rages on and on and on,
Like an undetected tumour.

COURTROOM CONFESSION

'Forgive me your honour, I am a sinner,
No human frame can get any thinner,
I robbed to buy some worldly joy,
That I've been deprived of since a boy,
But jail is no place for dinner.'

DARK NIGHTS

Windows closed, curtains drawn,
Darkness prowls as midnight's born.
At brothels bodies briskly bought,
Savings squandered for pleasure short.
Guilt fears the rays of dawn.

DECELERATE

Too much haste too much hurry,
Burdens man with unwanted worry.
Slow yet steady the race will win
Trade the scowl for a grin,
And pause the futile scurry.

DREAMS

Isn't it quite strange,
That dreams often change.
Desires are curtailed,
Failures artistically veiled.
When life is rearranged.

FATHER & SON

Nimble fingers toddler's talk,
When I crawled, he said 'walk'.
Now I run but he isn't happy,
I've even heard him say I'm 'Snappy'.
So, which of us is a gawk?

FROM THE OLD MAN AND THE SEA

Like Santiago and the marlin, whose skeleton came to shore,
Dream on and persist against all odds, never letting go.
The boat may be unlucky, the waters unluckier still,
Yet sharks can prey upon your catch not upon your will.
The old and wise have realised when to sail, when row.

FURY

A simpleton has no ounce of guile,
He's learned to wear a tolerant smile.
Tossed about by scheme and debt,
And when his clan is faced with threat,
His plainness turns hostile.

HAND OF GOD

Maradona had spectators awed,
Captaining the Argentinian squad.
And to his glee,
The referee didn't see,
The work of the Hand of God.

INSATIABLE

'Lend me some alms' was the beggar's cry,
'Buy me some food, lest from starvation I die'.
Moved by empathy I bought the beggar bread,
Eating it with gratitude the mendicant said,
'Can I have some wine; the bread is too dry.'

JOSEPH AND ADOLF

Joseph went out for a run,
And saw Adolf manslaughter for fun.
He suffered a stroke,
But Adolf that bloke,
Blew his brain out with a gun.

KANGAROO COURTS

Have you heard of an anecdote?
That minorities refrain to report.
Where inter caste wedlock hasn't scope,
And couples that choose to elope,
Face verdicts in a kangaroo court.

LAME EXCUSES

Betty bunked school one day,
So she cautiously planned what to say.
'Miss', she said, 'my grandpa died'.
"That quite spooky", the teacher replied ,
For his ghost was at the market yesterday.

LOCAL FAIRS

They still sell flutes at the local fairs and candy floss is still pink,
And penniless boys loiter aimlessly at lovely lasses to wink.
The merry-go-round is still here and so is the ring throwing game,
There's those key-chains of driftwood on which they carve your name.
But be careful of your wallet for the pickpocket is as quick as a blink.

LUST

Tracing her with his eyes; he unclothed her in his head,
Then barbarically seduced her to lie upon his bed.
She was just a teenager with bosoms still to bloom,
Oblivious at the arcade trying new perfume.
By her distant fragrance his fantasy was fed.

MEN OF WISDOM

Men of wisdom are men of might,
They differentiate wrong from right.
They wear gratitude like a cloak,
And respond to those that provoke,
In a tone sensitive and polite.

MS. FORTUNE

He got in to the team by luck,
And he was sure that fortune had struck.
But hey! What was that?
When he was sent to bat,
They got him out for a duck.

OLD MONK

At a barroom midst common flock,
With no restrictions by the clock.
Few drinks had set them cruising,
And it was quite amusing,
To watch the Old Monk talk.

PARTISANS

Are we being misled?
with criticism that's spread
by man of man to man
against creed and clan
for prejudice rules the head.

POLITICS

This turf is full of scandals,
Indifferent to protesting candles.
Mirrors shown to the opposition,
Yet! the layman is in no position,
To brave the wrath of vandals.

PROFESSIONALLY SPEAKING

The mason said, 'I lay the bricks to make a mighty wall',
'I fix the leaks' the plumber said, 'both big and small'.
The clergyman said, 'I preach righteousness over vice',
'I catch them all' said the exterminator, 'be it bugs or mice.'
'Someday' chuckled the undertaker, 'I will bury you all.'

PRUDENT TALK

Aye -aye Sir your always right,
Even when you call black, white.
You've all the answers, hold ever key,
To bail us out of misery,
And yet you're so polite.

RAINBOWS IN EVERY MAN

Have you felt blue; turned red,
Or simple stayed yellow in bed.
Have you gone green or blushed pink?
Then you will agree; I think,
A rainbow links the heart and head.

REJECTED

On day one he gave her a rose,
Day two he knelt to propose.
But with her knee,
She broke his teeth three,
A left him with a broken nose.

REPENT AT LEASURE

His mother warned, 'She's after money',
'Mum' he retorted 'your old and funny.'
In haste he married paying no heed,
And soon enough regretted the deed.
For now, he pays alimony.

ROLLING STONE

There's a kind of folk well known,
Who are always defensive of tone.
From responsibility they refrain,
Yet whine and complain,
And end up a rolling stone.

SCARS

It separates you from the crowd,
Those ugly scars pronounce aloud,
The pain, the suffering, the misery.
Conceal them not, let them be,
That's your story, wear it proud.

SUCH IS LIFE

Seldom grateful we oft complain,

And all our time is given to gain.

Such craving for the exemplary,

When life itself is temporary,

Like paper boats in the rain.

SUNDAY BREAKFAST

A sandwich of cheese and ham,

Doughnuts filled with raspberry jam.

A cup of coffee perfectly brewed,

A selfie to capture the food,

And post on Instagram.

THE MISER'S LADS

Not a dime he spent,

No matter where he went.

He died with coffers loaded,

They splurged all he hoarded,

On worthless merriment.

THE WALL

Tween East and West they built a wall,
And governed people by orders tall.
They weren't at war; They were just cold,
Countless died for being bold,
For it took 28 years for the fall.

THE SQUIRREL

Of the pair, an odd was found,
So, I frantically looked around.
I'd almost given up you see,
When the odd of socks suddenly,
Climbed up a tree on the playground.

TOLERABLE MAN

I think that I'm a tolerable man,
Silent and articulate in plan.
Rumours in the critic's voice,
Won't deter my choice,
To do every day what I can.

TYSON FURY

Tyson was known for his might,
People splurged to watch him fight.
But do you know of the twist,
That apart from his fist,
He also knew how to bite.

UNIQUE

Tom was tall and sleek,
With a ruddiness of cheek.
But his voice was so shrill,
It could give you the chill.
And that's what made him unique.

WAR

They are too blind to see,
That rage gives birth to misery.
An advance means no retreat,
For no army is taught 'defeat'.
Must corpses strew annexed territory?

WE'RE DIFFERENT

I said butter, he said jam,

I said eggs, he said ham.

I like coffee, he likes tea,

But that's quite ok you see,

For I am I and he is he.

WHEN MUM AND DAD FIGHT

I like it when mum and dad fight,

Though it doesn't seem very right.

They call each other names,

Play ignoring games.

Leaving me with my mobile all night.

WINTER COMES AGAIN

A clear sky, wintry sun, migratory birds in flight,

Festivity, weddings, picnics, bonfires burning bright.

Peanuts, Jaggery, Oranges, brewed coffee, and rum,

Fleece and Wool confirm that winter has come.

Another unfortunate vagrant succumbs to the night.